Growing in Peace

Childhood Wisdom for Children from Birth through Adolescence

June Williams

Madeline Denton, Illustrator

WestBow Press books may be ordered through booksellers or by contacting:

WestBow Press
A Division of Thomas Nelson & Zondervan
1663 Liberty Drive
Bloomington, IN 47403
www.westbowpress.com
844-714-3454

Interior Image Credit: Madeline Denton

ISBN: 978-1-6642-7993-3 (sc)
ISBN: 978-1-6642-7995-7 (hc)
ISBN: 978-1-6642-7994-0 (e)

Library of Congress Control Number: 2022918452

Print information available on the last page.

WestBow Press rev. date: 10/24/2022

WestBow
PRESS®
A DIVISION OF THOMAS NELSON
& ZONDERVAN

Dedicated to a Special Angel..........

The anticipation of new birth, excitement, love, abundant support~ these are the dreams of an infant joining a family here on earth. But what about those children who arrive in less than ideal circumstances~ children who are born into extreme poverty, children raised in highly dysfunctional families, children who lack support and guidance ~ is there any hope for these children?

The musical group, ALABAMA, highlights a famous hit song, "Angels Among Us". In their imagery, God has provided angels who "show us how to live, teach us how to give, and guide us with the light of love". From a Biblical point of view, we would refer to some of these angels as Proverbs 31 women. I have been privileged to know many such women in my life and one special lady from First Baptist Church of Inez, Kentucky, Mary McMasters.

There is a special place in heaven for women who have no children of their own but raise everyone's children. Mary is one of those angels who has adopted the children of Inez, working tirelessly to assist with their needs, physical, emotional and spiritual. She loves them, supports them, but most importantly, she shares with them about Jesus. Her example inspires all of us as we continue on our earthly journey. May we all aspire to be an "angel" in the life of a child as we nurture and help them to grow to be the people God envisions them to be!

My dearest child ~ welcome to the world!
How gracious of the Lord to loan you to us
for what we hope will be a lengthy visit.

Your mom and dad have been eagerly anticipating your arrival while the Lord has been preparing them to be the very best parents they can be.

Since you have arrived safely,
here are some words of wisdom
which we hope will make your
pathway a little less rocky as
you face some of the challenges
this new life will offer.

First about your parents: your
mom, dad, grandparents and
extended family members
can become some of the most
important people in your life
and deserve all the love and
respect you can give them.

Remember to love them, honor them, obey them and most importantly, to pray for them. The Lord has trusted them with the awesome responsibility of helping you to grow in His image. For optimum results, they will need His guidance.

Secondly, let's talk about others.
While your family will have a
profound influence on your young
life, your friends will do likewise.

Be kind to all human beings and all animals.
Listen with your heart as you interact with
others, always searching for the best in other
people: in highlighting the best in others, you
will discover the best you have to offer.

Remember that every human being offers new possibilities and new opportunities. Open your mind and heart to those who are different than you, remembering that each of us is a child of God with unique gifts to share.

Finally, some general tips to help you along the way. Remember that God sent you to earth with a particular purpose in mind. Always search for new ways to praise Him in every facet of your life.

Always live life to the fullest; every day is a gift from God so give every task your best effort, remembering that while we are all human, persistence builds character.

Have confidence in yourself and others.
We were all created in the image of God
so we must be pretty special.

Listen to your conscience;
obedience to that inner voice
can alleviate many heartaches
along the way.

Finally, and most
importantly, remember
your Creator, honoring
all of His Creation. Your
greatest happiness will
come from accepting
His love and following
His Will for your life.

Well little one, now that we have shared our wisdom, we welcome the wisdom that you bring us. God bless you and take care.

Printed in the United States
by Baker & Taylor Publisher Services